The Cicadas Are Coming!

Invasion of the periodical cicadas

Doug Wechsler

Wild Critter Press

Creepy Crawlers

On a warm spring night, an army of fearsome bugs burrows up out of the ground. Their curved claws swing back and forth. They creep across the ground. They clamber up trees. They stop and sink their claws into the bark. They look like creatures from a horror movie.

What is this invasion of bug-eyed insects? They are periodical cicada nymphs about to become adults. No one has seen them here for 17 years, probably long before you were born. Now millions of them are on the move. Where are these alien-looking creatures heading? Let's follow one.

Transformer Act

A nymph climbs to a safe height on the tree. It hooks its legs into the bark. Its body throbs, throbs, throbs. Suddenly, its exoskeleton splits. Now a "transformer" act begins. The soft, whitish insect inside molts, pushing itself out of the old "skin." Out comes the thorax and the head. Now its fiery red eyes really shine. It leans back to free its legs. It does a sit-up and crawls forward, pulling its abdomen out of the empty exoskeleton.

Head
Thorax
Abdomen

Ghostly Beginning

It rests on the tree trunk. The crinkled wings look useless. But the insect pumps blood into the veins inside its wrinkled wings. Like balloons, the wings blow up, unfold, and soon stretch beyond its body.

The pale, ghost-like body of the cicada slowly hardens. By morning, it becomes as black as the pupil in your eye.

The sun shines on the cicada, and the dark body heats quickly. With warm muscles it can fly! What would it be like to see the world after 17 years underground?

Enemies

Danger lurks everywhere. Almost every animal in the forest feasts on the hordes of cicadas. A bluebird brings a cicada back to the birdhouse. A little jumping spider gets a giant meal. A cicada falls to the surface of a pond and a fish gulps it down. There are so many cicadas that even after predators fill their bellies, swarms of them survive.

Built for the Band

Five days later, a male cicada starts singing. He is built like a musical instrument. His song comes from the timbals that sit beneath each wing. They act like the top of a drum. Muscles inside the cicada make the timbals pop in and out rapidly. The male cicada's abdomen is hollow. This makes his song louder, in the same way the hollow body of a guitar does.

cross-section of cicada (found dead)

Fun Fact
A cicada's ears are on its abdomen. The male buzzes so loud, he has flaps to cover his ears when he sings—or maybe he just doesn't like to hear himself sing?

timbal muscles

timbal

Annoying Tunes

Male cicadas do nothing except sing and fly, fly and sing. Thousands move around one tree. The ear-splitting chorus sounds like *wee-ooh, wee-ooh, wee-ooh*.... This endless cicada music can make some people go bonkers. The noise attracts more male cicadas to join in the racket. Females hear the song and come to find mates.

> **Fun Fact**
> If you run a lawnmower or power drill when there are lots of cicadas around, the buzzing noise might attract them, and they may land on you.

She Woos with Wings

A female answers the song. She flicks her wings and makes a sound like fingers snapping. A male hears this *click, click, click* and moves closer. He speeds up his song. She flicks again. He changes his tune: *whit, whit, whit*.... Then, they mate.

Sap Slurper

Later, the hungry female pushes her straw-like mouth into a twig. She sips sap from it. She has to drink lots of sap to get the nutrients she needs. Soon the sprinkle of cicada tinkle rains down from the tree.

mouth

mouth

egg slit

Hide the Eggs

Now for the cicada's last act, laying eggs. She pushes her egg-laying tube, the ovipositor, into a twig. With its jagged tip, she saws a slit. Eight eggs squeeze down the tube into the twig. She saws again and lays eight more next to the first batch. Shifting a bit up the twig, she repeats this again and again, and again. When she has laid about 500 eggs, she quits.

saw-tipped ovipositor from below

ovipositor

Recycling Cicadas

Soon after laying her last egg, the female cicada falls to the ground and dies. Her big job is done. The males have already died. Flies lay their eggs on the many cicada bodies. Ants feast as well. As the cicada bodies decompose, they fertilize the soil. The nutrients from their bodies seep down to the tree roots that will feed their nymphs when they hatch. Food that cicadas sipped from the trees is cycled back into the forest.

> **Fun Fact**
> Early settlers called periodical cicadas locusts, but they're not. Cicadas probably reminded them of the plagues of locusts in the Bible. Locusts are actually grasshoppers.

A Nymph Is Born

Inside the twigs, cicada nymphs form within the eggs. After eight weeks, a nymph the size of a tiny ant hatches. It quietly slips out of the slit in the twig and drops to the ground. Here, it is in danger. Before ants can attack, it digs quickly into the soil.

Fun Fact
Who needs eyes when you live underground? Cicadas are born with tiny black eyes. After they go underground and molt, they lose these and are blind.

egg

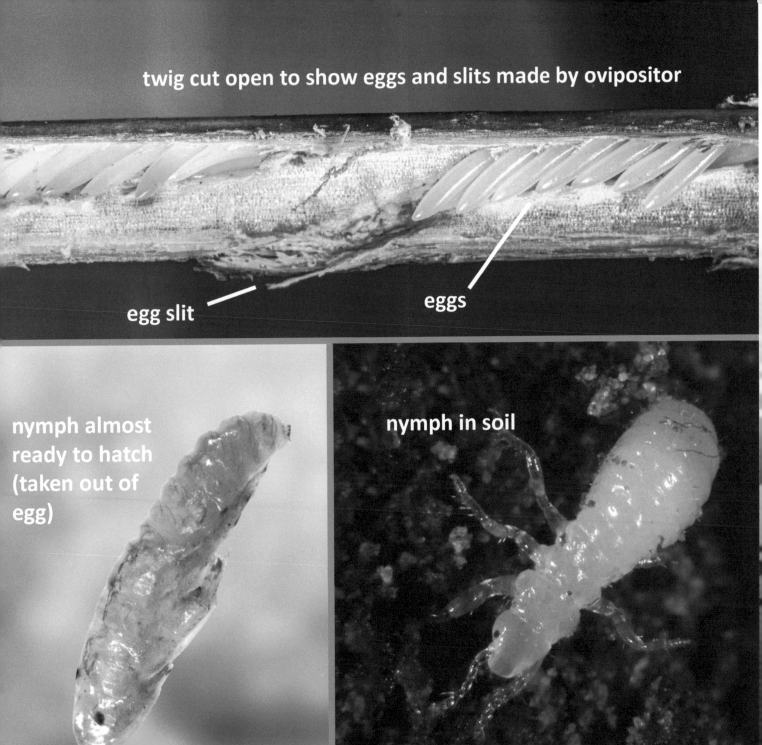

The Underworld

Underground now, the tiny nymph finds a grass root. It punctures the root with its mouth and drinks the juices. It grows very slowly. It does not need to hurry—it has 17 years to grow up.

The next spring, the slow-growing nymph has grown too big for its exoskeleton. It molts and sheds the old one. A new one hardens.

As the nymph grows, it digs deeper to feed from tree roots. Every three or four years, the nymph molts again and changes its shape.

A cicada nymph looks different after each molt.

End of a Cycle

Even underground, the nymph has enemies. A mole tunnels under the tree and eats hundreds of cicada nymphs. Fortunately, the mole never discovers *this* nymph.

It's now the spring of its 17th year. The nymph tunnels close to the surface. It waits there until . . .

. . . the soil warms to 64°F (18°C). This signals to the cicada that spring has come. It's time to *emerge!* The nymph climbs out of

its hole. It joins millions more as they crawl to the trees to molt, mate and meet their end.

CICADA FACTS

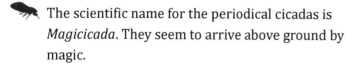 The scientific name for the periodical cicadas is *Magicicada*. They seem to arrive above ground by magic.

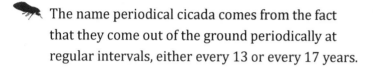 The name periodical cicada comes from the fact that they come out of the ground periodically at regular intervals, either every 13 or every 17 years.

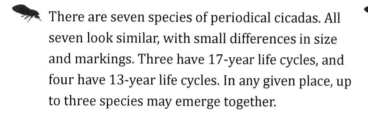 There are seven species of periodical cicadas. All seven look similar, with small differences in size and markings. Three have 17-year life cycles, and four have 13-year life cycles. In any given place, up to three species may emerge together.

Cicadas could not live without the bacteria in their abdomens that convert sap into the proteins they need for growth.

Periodical cicadas play an important role in their ecosystem. In years when periodical cicadas emerge, birds lay more eggs and raise more young.

Cicadas don't bite, don't sting, and are not poisonous to eat. Their defense is safety in numbers. So many cicadas emerge at once that predators can't eat them all.

Each species of periodical cicada makes its own distinct call.

Avoid using pesticides on lawns where cicadas live. Chemicals can kill the nymphs living underground.

Massospora fungus on cicada abdomen

Although periodical cicadas have many enemies, only one is known to be in sync with their life cycle—a fungus, *Massospora cicadina*. The fungus grows on the cicada's abdomen and prevents it from reproducing.

Some periodical cicadas synchronize their singing, making their choruses among the world's loudest insect noises.

In the best habitat, more than a million and a half cicadas come out of the ground in an area as small as a football field.

Periodical cicadas usually don't damage large, healthy trees. Twigs where they lay their eggs may die, but trees are not harmed. Spraying these harmless insects can wipe them out in a place where they have lived for many thousands of years. Young trees can be covered with netting for protection.

Cicada nymphs are not dormant underground, but grow very slowly.

GLOSSARY

abdomen (AB-dah-min): The third and last segment of an insect's body, behind the head and thorax.

decompose (DEE-com-pohz): To break up, decay, or rot.

emerge (ee-MERJ): To come out of something and into view, such as cicada nymphs emerging from the ground.

exoskeleton (ex-oh-SKEL-ah-tun): The tough, outer covering that an insect sheds as it grows or as it changes from nymph to adult.

molting (MOLT-ing): The process of shedding the exoskeleton.

nutrients (NEW-tree-ents): Substances that build and replenish the body.

nymph: (NIMF): The second stage of life in insects that have three life stages: egg, nymph, adult.

ovipositor (OH-vah-poz-eh-ter): A tube that extends from the rear of some female insects, through which eggs pass.

thorax (THOR-ax): The middle segment of an insect's body, between the head and the abdomen.

timbal (TIM-bull): The drum-like membrane on some insects that pops in and out to make noise.

BOOKS

Amstutz, Lisa J. *Cicadas*. Mankato, Minnesota: Capstone Press. 2013.

Buellis, Linda. *Cicadas (Dig Deep! Bugs That Live Underground)*. New York, New York: PowerKids Press. 2016.

Kritzky, Gene. *Periodical Cicadas*: The Brood X Edition. Columbus, Ohio: Ohio Biological Survey. 2021

Lawrence, Ellen. *A Periodical Cicada's Life*. New York, New York: Bearport Publishing. 2020

Pringle, Lawrence. *Cicadas!: Strange and Wonderful*. Honesdale, Pennsylvania: Boyds Mills Press. 2020.

Wechsler, Doug. *Bizarre Bugs*. Honesdale, Pennsylvania: Boyds Mills Press. 2003.

WEBSITES

www.cicadamania.com A wealth of information on all kinds of cicadas.

www.cicadasafari.org Help scientists research cicadas with the app at this site!

www.cicadas.uconn.edu Scientific site with information on periodical cicadas.

http://hydrodictyon.eeb.uconn.edu/projects/cicada/citizen/Dwyer_Simon_2014.pdf Field and lab studies for older students.

www.dougwechsler.com Read about cicadas, toads, the author, and his other engaging children's books.

Map of Periodical Cicada Broods

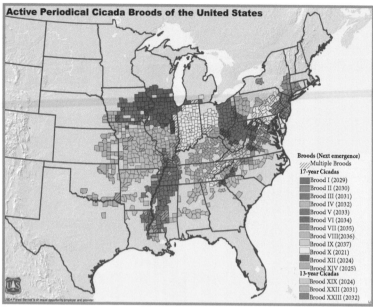

Active Periodical Cicada Broods of the United States

Broods (Next emergence)
- Multiple Broods

17-year Cicadas
- Brood I (2029)
- Brood II (2030)
- Brood III (2031)
- Brood IV (2032)
- Brood V (2033)
- Brood VI (2034)
- Brood VII (2035)
- Brood VIII (2036)
- Brood IX (2037)
- Brood X (2021)
- Brood XII (2024)
- Brood XIV (2025)

13-year Cicadas
- Brood XIX (2024)
- Brood XXII (2031)
- Brood XXIII (2032)

Forest Service map by A. M. Liebhold, M. J. Bohne, R. L. Liljag

This map shows where periodical cicadas will emerge each year. In any one place, they come out every 13 or 17 years. All 13-year cicadas or all 17-year cicadas that come out in a particular year belong to a brood. Scientists have numbered the broods with Roman numerals to keep track of them. In some places there are two broods, each on its own 13- or 17-year cycle.

Acknowledgements

Many thanks to Jessica Dimuzio, Michael Adams, and my wife Debbie Carr for helpful comments on the manuscript. Debbie also accompanied me on adventures in the field and encouraged me to self-publish this book. I am indebted to cicada expert Dr. Chris Smith who fact-checked the book. Annette DeGiovine, Elias P. Bonaros Jr., and Chris Simon kindly provided photographs of nymphs. Special thanks to Harold Underdown who edited the book and Kathie Klee who proofread it. I am grateful to the many generous people who supported my Kickstarter campaign to fund this project.

Text and photographs (except as noted below) Copyright © 2021 by Doug Wechsler

Additional photos:
Dwyer and Simon 2014. Experimental Studies of the Biology of 13- and 17-year Periodical Cicadas (see websites): cicada nymphs p. 23 bottom (2) and p. 24 top, p. 25 top; © **Annette DeGiovine & Elias P. Bonaros Jr.**: nymphs p. 24 bottom, 25 bottom; © **Illinois Department of Natural Resources**: mole p. 27.

Published by Wild Critter Press
Philadelphia PA 19118
www.dougwechsler.com/wildcritterpress

Library of Congress Control Number: 2021907298
ISBN 9781737021704 (hard cover)
ISBN 9781737021711 (soft cover)
ISBN 9781737021728 (ebook)
Library of Congress Cataloging-in-Publication Data is available.

About the Author

Doug Wechsler is an award-winning author and photographer of 24 books about natural science. He is a research associate at the Academy of Natural Sciences of Drexel University. He has observed wildlife around the world and in his backyard to bring the best stories to children and those young at heart. Giving presentations to audiences of all ages is one of his favorite things to do.

Learn about Doug at:
www.dougwechsler.com

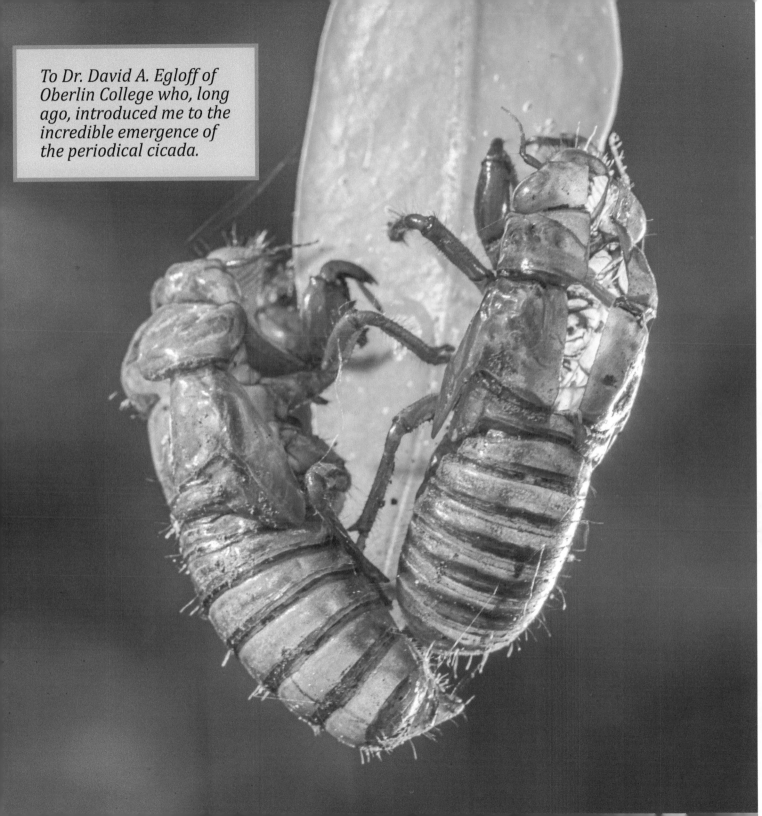

To Dr. David A. Egloff of Oberlin College who, long ago, introduced me to the incredible emergence of the periodical cicada.

CPSIA information can be obtained
at www.ICGtesting.com
Printed in the USA
BVHW020221170521
607533BV00002B/26